DASH Diet Recipes

Improve Your Health with Quick and Tasty Dash Recipes

<u>Anna Gray</u>

Table of Contents

Introduction

I would like to thank and congratulate you for getting this book, DASH Diet Recipes.

The DASH Diet was created by a branch of the US Department of Health and Human Services. DASH stands for Dietary Approaches to Stop Hypertension.

The DASH diet is a diet that was developed to help reduce high blood pressure. It is for this reason that the foods that can be consumed in this diet are low in sodium.
The diet is clear and simple:
- Consume more fruits, vegetables and low-fat dairy products.
- Reduce foods with high levels of trans fat, saturated fat and cholesterol.
- Consume foods with whole grains, seafood, nuts and poultry.
- Limit salt, red meat, sweets, and sugary drinks.
The safe strategy of the DASH diet is to minimize blood pressure without medicines.

We have researched and collected the most amazing Dash diet recipes that will help you improve your life in no time!

In this book you will discover simple and delicious meals you can make with the ingredients you're allowed to eat!

So, let's get this wonderful experience started! Have fun and enjoy the Dash lifestyle!

Chapter 1: Smoothies Recipes

1. Blueberry Smoothie

Preparation time: 10 minutes

Cook time: 5 minutes

Total time: 15 minutes

Serving: 2

Ingredients:

- One cup of spinach
- 2 cups of pineapple
- 4 cups of coconut water
- One cup of blueberries
- One medium apple
- 2 cups of watermelon

Instructions:

- Add all ingredients to a blender.
- Pulse it on high until smooth and creamy.
- Pour in a glass and enjoy it.

Nutrition per serving: Calories: 213 |Fat: 4.3 g |Carbohydrates: 10.4 g| Sugar: 17 g| Sodium: 48 mg| Fiber: 7.9 g |Protein: 5 g

2. Avocado Smoothie

Preparation time: 10 minutes

Cook time: 5 minutes

Total time: 15

Serving: 1

Ingredients:

- Cacao powder: 2 tbsp.

- Half avocado

- Half medium frozen banana

- Chia seeds: half teaspoon

- Plain almond milk: 1/4 cup

- Lime juice: 2 tbsp. optional

Instructions:

- Add all ingredients to a blender.

- Pulse it on high until smooth and creamy.

- Pour in a glass and enjoy it.

Nutrition per serving: Calories: 234 |Fat: 4.4 g |Carbohydrates: 12.3 g| Sugar: 16.4 g| Sodium: 53 mg| Fiber: 8.4 g |Protein: 5.6 g

3. Ultimate Fruit Smoothie

Preparation time: 10 minutes

Cook time: 10 mints

Total time: 20 mints

Servings: 1

Ingredients:

- 2 medium strawberries
- Half a cup of 2% milk
- Half mango, cut into chunks
- Half fresh peach sliced
- Half cup of orange juice
- ¼ cup of pineapple

Instructions:

- In a blender, add all ingredients
- Blend until smooth.
- Add more milk if required.
- Serve

Nutrition Per Serving: 225 calories| protein 5.8g |carbohydrates 46.4g |fat 3.1g| cholesterol 9.8mg |sodium 35.9mg

Chapter 2: Breakfast Recipes

1. Morning Quinoa

Preparation time: 10 minutes

Cook time: 14 Minutes

Total time: 24 minutes

Serving: 4

Ingredients:

- Cinnamon: ¼ teaspoon

- non-fat milk: 2 cups

- Dried currants: ¼ cup, chopped

- Uncooked quinoa: 1 cup

- Honey: ¼ cup

- Sliced almonds: ¼ cup

Instructions:

- Rinse quinoa and cook quinoa in boiled milk.

- Cook until milk is absorbed. Fluff with a fork.

- Add in the remaining ingredients and serve.

Nutrition per serving: 211 calories|12g carbohydrate |0 g saturated fat| 9 mg cholesterol| 6 g fat |77 mg sodium| 7g sugars|11 g protein|

2. Ezekiel Bread French Toast

Preparation time: 10 minutes

Cook time: 15 Minutes

Total time: 25

Serving: 2

Ingredients:

- Coconut Sugar: 2 Tbsp.

- Ezekiel Bread: 4 Slices

- Half Cup of Unsweetened Almond Milk

- Pinch of salt and cinnamon

- Stevia: 1 packet

- Vanilla:1 tsp

- Eggs: 2

Instructions:

- In a big bowl, add all ingredients but do not add bread yet. Mix well

- Soak bread in the mixture.

- On a greased pan, cook each piece of bread for five minutes until golden brown.

- Serve with syrup and enjoy!

Nutrition per serving: 167 calories|11.4 g carbohydrate |0 g saturated fat| 2 mg cholesterol| 3.2 g fat |45 mg sodium| 3g sugars|09 g protein|

3. Mushroom Shallot Frittata

Preparation time: 10 minutes

Cook time: 10 minutes

Total time: 20 minutes

Servings: 4

Ingredients:

- 4 shallots, chopped
- 2 cups of mushrooms, chopped
- Dried thyme: 1 teaspoon
- Parmesan cheese: ¼ cup grated
- Unsalted butter: 1 tablespoon
- 3 eggs and 5 whites
- Milk: 1 tablespoon
- Black pepper
- Fresh parsley: 2 teaspoons, chopped

Instructions:

- Let the oven preheat to 350 F
- Sauté shallots in butter for five minutes. Add thyme, mushroom, parsley, and black pepper.
- In a bowl, mix milk, eggs, cheese.

- Pour egg mix in a skillet over vegetables.

- When the eggs are set, bake for 15 minutes.

- Serve warm

Nutrition per serving: 222 calories|8.9 g carbohydrate |0 g saturated fat| 2.1 mg cholesterol| 5.5 g fat |55 mg sodium| 4 g sugars|12 g protein|

4. No-Bake Breakfast Granola Bars

Preparation time: 10 minutes

Cook time: 40 minutes

Total time: 50 minutes

Servings: 18

Ingredients:

- Half cup of peanut butter

- 2 and a half cups of toasted rice cereal

- Half cup of raisins

- Half cup of firmly packed brown sugar

- Vanilla: 1 teaspoon

- Half cup of light corn syrup

- Old fashioned oatmeal: 2 cups

Instructions:

- In a bowl, mix raisins, rice cereal, oatmeal. Mix with a wooden spoon.

- In a one-quart pan, mix corn syrup, brown sugar on medium flame. Mix constantly. Let it boil, then turn off the heat.

- Add in the sugar mix, vanilla, and peanut butter. Blend till smooth.

- Pour this mix over raisins and cereal. Mix well.

- In a baking pan, press this mixture and cool it, then cut into 18 bars.

Nutrition per serving: 215 calories|12.2g carbohydrate |0 g saturated fat| 0 mg cholesterol| 6.2 g fat |35 mg sodium| 3.4 g sugars|17 g protein|

5. Open Face Breakfast Sandwich

Preparation time: 10 minutes

Cook time: 14 Minutes

Total time: 24 minutes

Serving: 4

Ingredients:

- Four large eggs
- Four slices of whole-wheat bread
- Arugula: 2 cups
- Olive oil: 1 tablespoon
- 1 and a half teaspoons of lemon juice
- Ricotta cheese, part-skim: 3/4 cup
- Half teaspoon of salt, separated
- Fresh thyme chopped: 1 teaspoon
- Grated parmigiana cheese: 1/4 cup
- Black pepper: half tsp.

Instructions:

- Toast bread to your liking.
- In a bowl, mix arugula with 1/8 tsp. of salt, ¼ tsp. of pepper, two tsp of oil, and two tsp of lemon juice. Coat the arugula well.
- Cook eggs for two minutes in one tsp. of oil or until

whites are set. Set them aside

- In a bowl, add all cheeses, thyme, and two pinches of salt. Mix well.

- Add a layer of cheese mix, then arugula, and place an egg on top on a toast.

- Serve immediately.

Nutrition per serving: Serving: 1 toast Calories 263 | Carbohydrates: 19g | Protein: 17g | Fat: 15g | Saturated Fat: 6g | Cholesterol: 211mg | Sodium: 623mg | Fiber: 2g |

Chapter 3: Poultry & Meat Recipes

1. Chicken Chili with Sweet Potatoes

Preparation time: 10 minutes

Cook time: 40 minutes

Total time: 50 minutes

Serving: 5

Ingredients:

- Cooked chicken: 2 cups cut into half-inch cubes

- Extra-virgin olive oil: 2 tablespoons

- 3 cloves of minced garlic

- Sweet potato: 2 cups cut into cubes of half-inch

- One large chopped onion

- 1 diced green bell pepper

- Chili powder: 2 tablespoons

- 1/4 teaspoon of salt

- Dried oregano: 1 teaspoon

- 1 can of (15 ounces) cannellini beans, low-sodium, rinsed

- Ground cumin: 2 teaspoons

- Chicken broth, low-sodium: 2 cups

- 1 cup of frozen corn

- ¼ teaspoon of freshly ground black pepper

- Avocado, Sour cream, cilantro for garnish

Instructions:

- In a pot, sauté sweet potato, onion, bell pepper, and garlic in hot olive oil over medium flame. Cook for 5 to 6 minutes, until vegetables are tender.

- Add in cumin, chili powder, and oregano-cook for one minute.

- Add stock and beans. Let it boil. Reduce the flame, cover it partially, and let it simmer for 15 minutes.

- Turn the heat high, add in corn cook for one minute. Add chicken and cook for 1-2 minutes until heated through. Turn off the heat. Add in black pepper, salt.

- Garnish with avocado, sour cream, and cilantro, if you like.

Nutrition Per Serving: one and a half Cups: calories 324| dietary fiber 7.8g |protein 26g | cholesterol 48.2mg |carbohydrates 34.9g| other carbs 2.5| |sodium 369.6mg | fat 9.8g |saturated fat 1.7g | magnesium 87.2mg |potassium 792.6mg | sugars 5.4g|

2. Roasted Chicken Thighs with Peppers

Preparation time: 10 minutes

Cook time: 45 minutes

Total time: 55 minutes

Serving: 8

Ingredients:

- Extra virgin olive oil: 2 tablespoons, divided
- 6 cups of red potatoes, diced into one-inch pieces
- 2 green bell peppers, chopped into one-inch pieces
- Minced fresh thyme: 4 teaspoons
- 2 onions. Diced into one-inch pieces
- 8 skinless, boneless chicken thighs

- 2 sweet red peppers, chopped into one-inch pieces
- Chopped fresh rosemary: 3 teaspoons
- ¼ tsp. Of salt
- 1/4 teaspoon of freshly ground black pepper

Instructions:

- Let the oven preheat to 450 F.

- In a roasting pan, add all vegetables. Add one tbsp. of olive oil, two tbsp. of rosemary, thyme, and coat well.

- Put chicken thighs on top of vegetables.

- Drizzle the rest of the oil over the chicken and the rest of the rosemary, thyme. Sprinkle black pepper and salt over vegetables and chicken.

- Bake for 30 to 45 minutes, or until inserted thermometer in chicken reads 170.

- Serve right away and enjoy it.

Nutrition per chicken thigh + 1 cup of vegetables: calories 308|221mg sodium| 12g fat | 4g fiber |76mg cholesterol 24g protein|25g carbohydrate |3g saturated fat| 5g sugar

3. Apple-Cherry Pork Medallions

Preparation time: 10 minutes

Cook time: 30 minutes

Total time: 40 minutes

Serving: 4

Ingredients:

- Fresh thyme, minced: 1 teaspoon
- 1 pound of pork tenderloin
- 1/4 teaspoon of celery salt
- Extra virgin olive oil: 1 tablespoon
- One apple, cut into slices
- Cider vinegar: 1 tablespoon
- Fresh rosemary, minced: 1 teaspoon
- Apple juice, unsweetened: 2/3 cup
- Tart cherries, dried: 3 tablespoons
- One package of (8.8 ounces) brown rice, ready-to-serve
- Honey: 1 tablespoon

Instructions:

- Slice tenderloin into 12 pieces, crosswise. Season with celery salt, thyme, and rosemary.
- In a skillet, brown the pork on every side in olive, on medium flame. Take out the pork.

- In the same pan, add cherries, vinegar, honey, apple juice, and apple. Let it boil. Scrape the browned bits turn the heat low, let it simmer uncovered for 3 to 4 minutes until apples become tender.

- Add pork into pan, coat with sauce, cook for 3 to 4 minutes, until meat is tender.

- Cook rice as per instructions.

- Serve on the side of pork tenderloin.

Nutrition per serving: calories 372|288 mg sodium| 11g fat |2g sugars |4g saturated fat| 32 mg cholesterol |3g fiber|31g protein|| 34g carbohydrate

4. Asparagus Turkey Stir-Fry

Preparation time: 10 minutes

Cook time: 20 minutes

Total time: 30 minutes

Serving: 4

Ingredients:

- 1 pound of turkey breast tenderloins, sliced into half-inch strips
- 4 cups of trimmed fresh asparagus, slice into one and a half-inch piece
- 1/4 cup of low sodium chicken broth
- Corn-starch: 2 teaspoons

- Lemon juice: 1 tablespoon
- 1 clove of minced garlic
- Extra virgin olive oil: 2 tablespoons
- Low sodium soy sauce: 1 teaspoon
- One jar of (2 ounces) pimientos, sliced and drained

Instructions:

- In a bowl, mix broth, soy sauce, lemon juice, and corn starch, set it aside.

- In a skillet, sauté garlic and turkey in one tbsp. of oil, until meat is no longer pink, take out the turkey and keep it warm.

- In the remaining oil, sauté asparagus till tender, crispy, add pimientos. Add broth mixture to the pan, cook for 60 seconds, or until it becomes thick.

- Add turkey to pan, heat well, and serve with warm rice.

Nutrition per serving: 1 and 1/4 cups: calories 205| 204mg sodium|9g fat |56mg cholesterol| 28g protein |5g carbohydrate| 1g saturated fat| 1g sugars|1g fiber

5. Chicken & Goat Cheese Skillet

Preparation time: 10 minutes

Cook time: 20 minutes

Total time: 30 minutes

Serving: 2

Ingredients:

- Half pound of skinless, boneless chicken breasts, slice into one-inch pieces
- Extra virgin olive oil: 2 teaspoons
- 1/4 teaspoon of salt
- Freshly cooked pasta or rice
- Fresh goat cheese, herbed: 2 tablespoons crumbled
- Trimmed fresh asparagus: 1 cup cut into one-inch pieces
- Three diced tomatoes
- 2% milk: 3 tablespoons
- 1/8 teaspoon of black pepper
- 1 clove of minced garlic

Instructions:

- Season chicken breast with pepper and salt. In a pan, cook chicken in hot olive oil for 4 to 6 minutes or until cooked, turn off the heat keep warm in a warm oven.

- In a pan, add asparagus, sauté over medium flame, over

one minute, then add garlic cook for thirty seconds.

- Add in milk, 2 tbsp. Cheese, and tomatoes, cover it, and cook for 2 to 3 minutes until cheese starts to melt. Add in chicken.

- Serve on the side of cooked pasta or rice.

Nutrition per serving: 1 and a half cups of chicken mixture: calories 251|74mg cholesterol| 11g fat |29g protein|3g saturated fat| 447mg sodium|5g sugars| 3g fiber |8g carbohydrate |

6. Chicken Veggie Packets

Preparation time: 10 minutes

Cook time: 30 minutes

Total time: 40 minutes

Serving: 4

Ingredients:

- 4 skinless, boneless chicken breasts, cut into halves

- Half cup of sweet red pepper: cut into julienne style

- Pearl onions: 1 cup

- 1 and a half cups of baby carrots

- 1/4 teaspoon of black pepper

- 2 cups of fresh mushrooms, sliced

- Fresh thyme, minced: 3 teaspoons

- Lemon wedges for serving

Instructions:

- Let the oven preheat to 375 F.

- Pound the chicken breast to half an inch of thickness.

- Place chicken on the bottom in a large foil paper, add red pepper, mushrooms, onions, and carrots on top. Sprinkle black pepper, thyme, a pinch of salt, if you like.

- Fold the foil around vegetables and chicken.

- Bake on a baking sheet for 20 minutes or more if required.

- Serve with lemon wedges.

Nutrition per serving: calories 175| 11g carbohydrate|3g fat | 63mg cholesterol| 1g saturated fat|100mg sodium| 2g fiber| 25g protein|6g sugars|

7. Chicken Chop Suey

Preparation time: 10 minutes

Cook time: 35 minutes

Total time: 45 minutes

Serving: 6

Ingredients:

- One pound of skinless, boneless chicken breasts, slice into one-inch cubes

- Half teaspoon of dried tarragon

- Cooked hot brown rice: 3 cups

- Half teaspoon of dried basil

- Extra virgin olive oil: 4 teaspoons

- 1 cup of pineapple, unsweetened, drained but reserve the juice

- Half teaspoon of dried marjoram

- 1 and a half cups of chopped carrots

- One can of (8 ounces) water chestnuts, sliced and drained

- Teriyaki sauce, reduced-sodium: 3 tablespoons

- One diced tart apple

- Corn-starch: 2 tablespoons

- Half teaspoon of lemon zest, grated

- Half cup of diced onion

- 1 cup of cold water

- 3 tablespoons of pineapple juice, unsweetened

Instructions:

- In a large skillet, add olive oil, sauté lemon zest, chicken, and herbs on medium flame. Cook until browned but slightly.

- Add rest of the ingredients except for corn-starch and water, but add ¾ cup of water, teriyaki sauce, and pineapple juice.

- Let it boil, turn the heat low and let it simmer, for 10 to 15 minutes, covered, till chicken is cooked through.

- Mix water with corn-starch. Slowly add in the chicken. Let it simmer until it becomes thick, for two minutes.

- Serve on the side of brown rice.

Nutrition per serving: one cup: calories 302|237mg sodium|7g fat | 63mg cholesterol| 1g saturated fat|34g carbohydrate |5g fiber| 20g sugars| |25g protein

Chapter 4: Fish & Seafood Recipes

1. Salmon Parcels with Wild Rice, Pesto

Preparation time: 10 minutes

Cook time: 20 minutes

Total time: 30 minutes

Servings: 2

Ingredients:

- Salmon fillets: one cup

- Rice: one cup

- Red pesto: 3 tablespoons

- One lemon: half juiced and half thinly sliced

- Purple sprouting broccoli: half cup

- Black olives chopped: 2 tablespoons

- Basil

Instructions:

- Let the oven overheat till 200 C. line the baking tray with parchment paper. Separate the mixed grains and rice. Stir in the lemon juice, olives, 2 tablespoon of pesto, and half of the basil. Mix well, put in the centre of the baking tray

- Place the salmon over the grains and scatter over each fillet the remaining pesto. Cover with the slices of lemon and broccoli, then cover with parchment paper on top. make it a packet around filling

- Roast for about half an hour in the oven till broccoli is soft and salmon is completely cooked

- Serve with basil on top.

Nutrition Per Serving: 361 calories| total fat 16.2 g | carbohydrates 18 g| protein 9 g | Cholesterol 5.1 mg| Sodium 114 mg| potassium 121 mg| Phosphorus 109 mg |Calcium 56 mg| Fiber 3.2 g

2. Salmon with Green Bean Pilaf

Preparation time: 10 minutes

Cook time: 20 minutes

Total time: 30 minutes

Servings: 4

Ingredients:

- Olive oil: 3 tbsp.
- Pre-cooked white rice: one cup
- Wild salmon: 1 & ¼ pound (skinned and cut into four pieces)
- Green beans and cut into thirds: 12 ounces
- Low-fat Mayonnaise: 2 tbsp.
- Minced garlic: one tbsp.
- Pine nuts: 2 tbsp.
- Water: 2 tbsp.
- Salt: 1/4 tsp.
- Ground pepper: half tsp.
- Parsley
- Whole-grain mustard: 2 tsp.
- One lemon: zested, cut into wedges

Instructions:

- Let the oven pre-heat till 425 F.

- Place parchment paper on baking sheet

- Brush the salmon with one spoonful of oil and place them on the baking sheet.

- Mash the salt and garlic together. In a small bowl, combine one teaspoon of the garlic paste with mustard, mayonnaise, 1/4 teaspoon of pepper.

- Spread the blend over the fish.

- Roast the salmon until it flakes easily—six-eight minutes per inch of thickness.

- Heat the remaining two spoons of oil over medium flame in a skillet.

- Add lemon zest, green beans, pine nuts, leftover garlic paste, and black pepper; stir for almost four minutes until the beans are soft.

- Reduce to medium heat. Add the rice and water and cook for three minutes, stirring, until hot.

- Serve with green beans and lemon and top with parsley.

Nutrition Per Serving: 242 calories| total fat 17.1 g | carbohydrates 18.1 g| protein 21.1 g | Cholesterol 6.1 mg| Sodium 125 mg| potassium 113 mg| Phosphorus 127 mg |Calcium 56 mg| Fiber 2.1 g

3. Fish Tacos with Broccoli Slaw & Cumin Sour Cream

Preparation time: 10 minutes

Cook time: 20 minutes

Total time: 30 minutes

Serving: 4

Ingredients:

- Eight tortillas

- Fish sticks: 2 10-oz. Packages

- Half red onion sliced

- Two limes, juiced and wedges

- Broccoli: 12 ounces

- Kosher salt: half tsp.

- Olive oil: 2 tablespoons

- Half cup of sour cream

- Cilantro: 1 cup

- Half tsp. of ground cumin

Instructions:
- According to the direction on the package, cook the fish sticks.

- Chop broccoli' heads. Peel the stalks and cut them into matchsticks.

- In a large bowl, add the lime juice, onion, and ¾ teaspoon of salt.; mix and set aside around ten minutes.

- Add broccoli stalks and tops, oil, cilantro, and mix

- Mix

- cumin, sour cream, and salt in a small dish. Serve with fish

Nutrition Per Serving: two tacos each: 227 calories| total fat 14 g | carbohydrates 12.5 g| protein 20.3 g | Cholesterol 7.1 mg| Sodium 120 mg| potassium 109 mg| Phosphorus 102 mg |Calcium 6.1 mg| Fiber 3 g

4. Roasted Salmon with Smoky Chickpeas & Greens

Preparation time: 10 minutes

Cook time: 20 minutes

Total time: 30 minutes

Serving: 4

Ingredients:

- Wild salmon: 1 and ¼ pounds, cut into 4 pieces

- Chopped kale: 10 cups

- Olive oil: 2 tbsp.

- Salt: ¼ tsp.

- Can of chickpeas: 15 ounces

- Garlic powder: ¼ tsp.

- Buttermilk: 1/3 cup

- Low-fat Mayonnaise: ¼ cup

- Smoked paprika: one tbsp.

- Water: ¼ cup

- Ground pepper: half tsp.

- Chives: ¼ cup

Instructions:

- let the oven pre-heat 'til 425 F and put the racks in the upper third portion, middle of the oven

- In a bowl, add one spoon of paprika, oil, 1/4 tsp of salt.

- Dry the chickpeas and mix with the paprika blend, put them on a baking sheet, and bake for half an hour on the upper rack.

- In the food, blender adds puree buttermilk, basil, mayonnaise,1/4 tsp of pepper, and garlic powder pulse till creamy. Set it aside.

- Heat a skillet, add one tablespoon of oil over medium flame.

- Add the kale, cook for two minutes. Add water and keep cooking, around five minutes until the kale is soft.

- Remove from flame, and add salt to the dish.

- Take out the chickpeas from the oven, transfer them to one side of the pan. Place the salmon on the other hand, and season with salt and pepper.

- Bake for 5- 8 minutes until the salmon is completely cooked.

- Top with dressing, herbs, and serve with kale and chickpeas.

Nutrition Per Serving: 247 calories| total fat 13.2 g | carbohydrates 14.2 g| protein 24 g | Cholesterol 5.3 mg| Sodium 123 mg| potassium 133 mg| Phosphorus 109 mg |Calcium 56 mg| Fiber 3.1 g

5. Greek Roasted Fish with Vegetables

Preparation time: 10 minutes

Cook time: 20 minutes

Total time: 30 minutes

Serving: 4

Ingredients:

- Four skinless salmon fillets: 5-6 ounces

- Two red, yellow, orange sweet peppers, cut into rings

- Five cloves of garlic chopped

- Sea salt: 1/4 tsp.

- Olive oil: 2 tbsp.

- Black pepper: half tsp

- Pitted halved olives: ¼ cup

- One lemon

- Parsley: 1 and ½ cups

- Finely snipped fresh oregano:1/4 cup

Instructions:

- Let the oven preheat to 425 F

- Put the potatoes in a bowl. Drizzle 1 spoon of oil, sprinkle with salt and garlic. Mix well, shift to the baking pan, cover with foil. Roast them for half an hour

- In the meantime, thaw the salmon. Combine the sweet peppers, parsley, oregano, olives, salt (few pinches) and pepper in the same bowl. Add one tablespoon of oil, mix well.

- Wash salmon and dry it with paper towels. Sprinkle with Black pepper, and top of it, salmon. Uncover it and roast for ten minutes or till salmon starts to flake.

- Add lemon zest and lemon juice over salmon and vegetables. Serve hot

Nutrition Per Serving: 278 calories| total fat 12 g | carbohydrates 9.2 g| protein 15.4 g | Cholesterol 7.1 mg| Sodium 131 mg| potassium 141 mg| Phosphorus 121 mg |Calcium 56 mg| Fiber 3.4 g

Chapter 5: Appetizer, Sides & Snacks Recipes

1. Southwestern Potato Skins

Preparation time: 10 minutes

Cook time: 30 minutes

Total time: 40 minutes

Serving: 12

Ingredients:

- Extra virgin olive oil: 1 teaspoon

- 1 chopped tomato

- Chili powder: 1 teaspoon

- Hot pepper sauce: 1/8 teaspoon

- Baking potatoes: 6 larges

- Half cup of cheddar cheese, shredded

- Turkey bacon: 6 slices, crispy cooked, chopped

- Green onions: 2 tablespoons cut into slices

Instructions:

- Let the oven preheat to 450 F. spray oil on a baking sheet.

- Wash and pat dry potatoes; with a fork, pierce them all over.

- Microwave for ten minutes, on high, uncovered until tender.

- Cool the potatoes, cut into half, and take out the middle part and leave some of it.

- In another bowl, mix hot sauce, olive oil, and chili powder.

- Pour this chili mixture inside of potatoes inside. Cut in further half.

- In a bowl, mix bacon with onions and tomatoes. Fill the potatoes with this mixture and top with cheese.

- Bake for ten minutes, until cheese melts.

- Serve right away and enjoy it.

Nutrition per serving: two crispy skins: 194 Calories | Dietary fiber 6 g| Sodium 164 mg| Total fat 6 g| Monounsaturated fat 2 g| Cholesterol 20 mg| Saturated fat 3 g| Total sugars 2 g| Total carbohydrate 27 g| Protein 8 g

2. Roasted Red Pepper Hummus

Preparation time: 10 minutes

Cook time: 10 minutes

Total time: 20 minutes

Serving: 16

Ingredients:

- Fresh lemon juice: 1 tablespoon

- Red bell pepper, roasted: 1 cup cut into slices, remove seeds

- Low sodium onion powder: 1 teaspoon

- White sesame seeds: 2 tablespoons

- 2 cups of cooked chickpeas

- Extra virgin olive oil: 1 tablespoon

- 1 and 1/4 teaspoons of cumin

- ¼ tsp. Of kosher salt

- Cayenne pepper: 1/4 teaspoon

- Low sodium garlic powder: 1 teaspoon

Instructions:

- Place all ingredients in a food processor. Pulse on high until smooth.

- Serve with baked pita chips.

Nutrition per serving: 3 tbsp.: 53 Calories | Total carbohydrate 7 g| Total fat 2 g| Saturated fat 0 g| Monounsaturated fat 1 g| Dietary fiber 2 g| Sodium 126 mg| Total sugars 1 g| Protein 2 g| Cholesterol 0 mg|

3. Spanakopita Bites

Preparation time: 10 minutes

Cook time: 25 minutes

Total time: 35 minutes

Serving: 4

Ingredients:

- 4 sheets phyllo dough

- Baby spinach leaves: 2 cups

- Grated Parmesan cheese: 2 tablespoons

- Low-fat, cottage cheese: 1/4 cup

- Dried oregano: 1 teaspoon

- Water: 2 tablespoons

- One egg white only

- Lemon zest: 1 teaspoon

- Cayenne pepper; 1/8 teaspoon

- Olive oil: 1 tablespoon

- Kosher salt: few pinches and freshly ground black pepper: 1/4 teaspoon

Instructions:

- In a pot over high heat, add water and spinach, cook until wilted.

- Drain it and cool for ten minutes. Squeeze out excess moisture.

- In a bowl, mix cottage cheese, Parmesan cheese, oregano, salt, cayenne pepper, egg white, freshly ground black pepper, spinach, and zest. Mix it well or in the food processor.

- Lay one phyllo sheet on a flat surface. Spray with oil. Add the second sheet of phyllo on top—spray oil. Add a total of 4 oiled sheets.

- Form 16 strips from these four oiled sheets. Add one tbsp. of filling in one strip. Roll it around filling.

- Spray the baking sheet with oil. Put bites in the tray, spray with oil. Cook for 15-20 minutes at 375°F until crispy and golden brown. Flip halfway through.

- Serve with leaner protein.

Nutrition per serving: 2 bites: Calories 82|Fat 4g| Sodium 103 mg| Protein 4g| Dietary fiber 2g| Total fat 4g| Carbohydrate 7g| Cholesterol 5 mg| Protein 2 g| Saturated fat 2g|

4. Pickled Asparagus

Preparation time: 10 minutes

Cook time: 10 minutes

Total time: 20 minutes

Serving: 6

Ingredients:

- 1 cup of water
- 1 pound of trimmed asparagus, fresh
- White wine vinegar: 1/4 cup
- Cider vinegar: 1/4 cup
- 1 sprig of fresh dill
- Pearl onions: 1/4 cup
- 8 black peppercorns, whole
- 2 cloves, whole
- Red pepper flakes: 1/4 teaspoon
- 3 garlic cloves, whole
- 6 coriander seeds, whole

Instructions:

- Trim the asparagus, wash and pat dry, cut in the same size as would fit in a jar.
- Trim the onion if required.

- Add all ingredients to an airtight jar. Keep in the refrigerator for four weeks.

Nutrition per serving: ½ of a cup: Calories 24|Total carbohydrate 4 g| Sodium 5 mg| Total sugars 2 g| Saturated fat Trace| Dietary fiber 2 g| Total fat Trace| Protein 2 g| Cholesterol 0 mg|

Chapter 6: Vegetarian & Meatless Recipes

1. Vegetable, Lentil, & Garbanzo Bean Stew

Preparation time: 10 minutes

Cook time: 2 hours

Total time: 2 hours 10 minutes

Serving: 8

Ingredients:

- 3 cups of butternut squash, remove seeds, peeled, cut into one-inch-thick cubes
- 3 large-sized carrots, peeled and slice into half-inch thick pieces
- 3 cloves of minced garlic
- Tomato paste, no-added-salt: 2 tablespoons
- Vegetable stock, low-sodium: 4 cups
- 1 teaspoon of freshly ground black pepper
- 1 cup of red lentils, sorted and rinsed
- 1 can of (16 ounces) garbanzo beans, rinsed and drained
- 2 teaspoons of ground cumin

- Two large-sized onions, finely chopped
- 1 teaspoon of turmeric
- 1/4 teaspoon of saffron
- Half cup of fresh cilantro, finely chopped
- Peeled & minced fresh ginger: 2 tablespoons
- 1/4 cup of fresh lemon juice
- Half cup of finely chopped unsalted peanuts, roasted

Instructions:

- In a Dutch oven, sauté squash, onions, garlic, carrots over medium flame, or onions start to brown.

- Add in vegetable stock, clean the pan of browned bits.

- Add seasonings, lentils, and tomato paste. Cover it and cook for one and half hours on medium heat until squash and lentils are soft. Or cook in a slow cooker for 4 to 6 hours on low.

- Stir occasionally. Add in garbanzo beans and lemon juice. Serve warm right away, top with cilantro and chopped peanuts.

Nutrition per serving: About 2 cups: 287 Calories | Total carbohydrate 41g| Total fat 7g| Trans-fat 0 mg| Monounsaturated fat 3g| Saturated fat 1g| Cholesterol 0 mg| Dietary fiber 9 g| Added sugars 0g| Sodium 258 mg| Protein 13g

2. Pepper Ricotta Primavera

Preparation time: 10 minutes

Cook time: 20 minutes

Total time: 30 minutes

Serving: 6

Ingredients:

- Half cup of milk, fat-free
- 1 green pepper, medium-sized, cut into julienne
- Extra virgin olive oil: 4 teaspoons
- 1 zucchini, medium-sized, cut into slices
- 1 clove of minced garlic

- Half teaspoon of red pepper flakes, crushed
- 1 cup of ricotta cheese, part-skim
- 1 sweet red pepper, medium-sized, cut into julienne
- 1/4 teaspoon of dried basil
- 1 sweet yellow pepper, medium-sized, cut into julienne
- Frozen peas, 1 cup, thawed
- One cup of fettuccine, cooked and drained
- 1/4 teaspoon of dried oregano

Instructions:

- In a bowl, mix milk and cheese set it aside.
- In a large pan, add olive oil on medium flame. Add pepper flakes and garlic cook for one minute. Add all vegetables, other seasonings, cook until tender-crisp for almost five minutes.
- Add milk-cheese to cooked pasta, add cooked vegetables on top.
- Mix well.
- Serve right away and enjoy it.
- Garnish with parmesan cheese.

Nutrition per serving: 1 cup: calories 229|31g carbohydrate| 7g fat |3g saturated fat| | 11g protein| 88mg sodium|6g sugars| 13mg cholesterol| 4g fiber

3. Tuscan White Bean Stew

Preparation time: 10 minutes

Cook time: 60 minutes

Total time: 70 minutes

Serving: 4

Ingredients:

For the croutons:

- 1 slice of bread, whole-grain, cut into half-inch-thick cubes
- 2 cloves of garlic, cut into quarters
- Extra-virgin olive oil: 1 tablespoon

For the soup:

- One bay leaf
- 2 cups of dried cannellini beans or white beans, sorted, rinsed, and soaked overnight, must be drained
- Yellow onion, roughly chopped: 1 cup
- 6 cups of water
- 1/8 teaspoon of salt, divided
- Extra virgin olive oil: 2 tablespoons
- 6 cloves of minced garlic

- 3 carrots, medium-sized, peeled and roughly chopped

- 1 and a half cups of vegetable stock, low sodium, or broth

- 1 tablespoon of fresh rosemary, finely chopped and 6 more sprigs

- 1/4 teaspoon of freshly ground black pepper

Instructions:

- In a pan, add olive oil, and garlic cook for one minute, on medium flame. Turn off the heat and let it cool for ten minutes to make garlic-infused olive oil. Take out the garlic. Turn on the heat to medium flame.

- Add pieces of bread, and cook for 3-5 minutes. Keep stirring until they become crispy.

- Take out in a bowl. Set them aside.

- In a soup pot, add beans, bay leaf, salt, and water. Let it boil on high flame.

- Turn the heat to low, cover it partially, and let it simmer for 60-75 minutes or until the beans are soft.

- Reserve half of a cup cooking liquid. Drain the beans, take out the bay leaf.

- Take out the cooked beans in a large bowl, set them aside.

- In a bowl, add reserved liquid, half a cup of beans. Make a paste by mashing them. Mix the cooked beans with mashed beans

- In the pot, add olive oil, sauté onion, and carrots on medium flame, for 6-7 minutes until carrots are tender-crisp. Add in garlic cook for one minute.

- Add in the chopped rosemary, salt, bean mixture, pepper, and stock. Let it boil, turn the heat to low, and let it simmer for five minutes until everything is heated well.

- Add hot stew in bowls, top with crispy croutons, sprigs of rosemary, and serve right away.

Nutrition per serving: About 1 and 1/4 cups of stew + 1/6 of the croutons: Calories 307| Monounsaturated fat 5 g| Total carbohydrate 45 g| Sodium 334 mg| Dietary fiber 11 g| Saturated fat 1 g| Cholesterol 0 mg| Protein 16 g| Total sugars 3 g| Total fat 7 g|

4. Vegetarian Chili

Preparation time: 10 minutes

Cook time: 30 minutes

Total time: 40 minutes

Serving: 8

Ingredients:

- 2 cloves of minced garlic
- 1 cup of finely diced celery
- 8 cups of crushed tomatoes
- 1 cup of finely chopped green bell pepper
- 2 cups of finely chopped onion

- Water: 2 tablespoons

- 2 cups of cooked pinto beans, rinsed, no salt added, drained

- 2 Fresno peppers, finely diced

- 2 tablespoons of ground cumin

- 1 tablespoon of smoked paprika or chipotle pepper

- 1 tablespoon of balsamic vinegar, no salt added

- Dried oregano: 1 tablespoon

- 1 tablespoon of freshly ground black pepper

Instructions:

- In a large pot, add onion, garlic, 2 tbsp. of water, bell pepper, and celery cook on low heat for ten minutes, until onion turns translucent.

- Add the rest of the ingredients, cover it, and let it simmer for 1 to 2 hours. Stir occasionally.

- If chili is too thick, add water to get your desired consistency.

Nutrition per serving: About 2 cups: Calories 161| Total carbohydrate 31 g| Sodium 116 mg| Dietary fiber 10 g| Total fat 1 g| Trans-fat 0 g| Cholesterol 0 mg| Protein 7 g| Saturated fat Trace| Total sugars 11 g |Monounsaturated fat 1 g| Added sugars 0 g|

5. Pumpkin soup

Preparation time: 10 minutes

Cook time: 40 minutes

Total time: 50 minutes

Serving: 4

Ingredients:

- 3/4 cup of water, divided
- 1 can of (15 ounces) pumpkin puree, low sodium
- 1 green onion, top only, finely chopped
- 2 cups of unsalted homemade vegetable broth
- 1 cup of fat-free milk
- 1 small-sized onion, finely chopped
- half teaspoon of ground cinnamon
- 1/4 teaspoon of ground nutmeg
- 1/8 teaspoon of freshly ground black pepper

Instructions:

- In a large pan, add ¼ cup of water on medium flame. Add onions, and cook for three minutes until soft. Do not dry the onions completely.
- Add the rest of the water, nutmeg, broth, pumpkin, and cinnamon. Mix well and let it boil, turn the heat to low, let it simmer for five minutes. Add in milk, mix well. Do not let it boil.

- Add soups into bowls, sprinkle crushed black pepper, slices of green onion.

- Serve right away and enjoy it.

Nutrition per serving: About 1 cup: Calories 77| Total carbohydrate 14 g| Sodium 57 mg| Total fat 1 g| Trans-fat 0 g| Saturated fat Trace| Cholesterol 1 g| Dietary fiber 4 g| Monounsaturated fat 1 g| Added sugars 0 g| Protein 3 g|

6. Grilled Portobello Mushroom Burgers

Preparation time: 10 minutes

Cook time: 30 minutes

Total time: 40 minutes

Serving: 4

Ingredients:

- 1 tablespoon of honey or sugar

- 1/3 cup of low sodium balsamic vinegar

- 4 slices of thin tomato

- 4 large-sized, Portobello mushroom only caps, stems removed

- Half cup of water

- 1 clove of minced garlic

- Cayenne pepper: 1/4 teaspoon, it is optional

- 4 slices of red onion

- Extra virgin olive oil: 2 tablespoons

- 2 lettuce leaves, cut into halves

- Four toasted whole-wheat buns

Instructions:

- Clean and pat dry the mushrooms, trim them, and put in a baking dish, cap side down.

- In a small bowl, mix the honey, cayenne pepper, vinegar, olive oil, garlic, and water.

- Pour this marinade over mushrooms. Cover with plastic wrap and keep in the refrigerator for about 60 minutes, turning mushrooms halfway over.

- Preheat the charcoal grill, or broiler or gas grill

- Coat the grill with oil spray away 4-6 inches from heat source.

- Broil or grill mushrooms on medium flame, keep turning, cook until soft for five minutes on every side.

- Baste with the marinade so mushrooms would not dry out. Take them out on a serving plate.

- Add one grilled mushroom on a toasted bun with slices of onion and tomatoes, and lettuce leaf. Serve right away.

Nutrition per serving: one burger: Calories 273| Total carbohydrate 39 g| Saturated fat 21 g| Dietary fiber 6 g| Cholesterol 0 mg| Total fat 9 g| Sodium 262 mg| Protein 9 g| |Added sugars 3 g| Total sugars 11 g| Monounsaturated fat 5 g|

Chapter 7: Soups & Salad Recipes

1. Beans & Tuna Salad

Preparation time: 10 minutes

Cook time: 15 minutes

Total time: 25 minutes

Serving: 4

Ingredients:

- Half baguette, whole-grain, cut into 2-inch pieces
- Two dill pickles, small, cut into one-inch pieces

- Olive oil: 2 tablespoons

- One can of (16 ounces) beans, rinsed, no salt added

- One can of (7 ounces) water-packed tuna, drained, no salt added

- Half cup of red onion, sliced

- Black pepper: 1/4 teaspoon

- Fresh parsley chopped: 2 tablespoons

- Red wine vinegar: 2 tablespoons

Instructions:

- Let the broiler preheat. Add baguette pieces on a baking tray drizzle with one tbsp. of oil and toss well. Broil for 1-2 minutes, till crispy and golden.

- In a bowl, add onion, beans, oil, pickles, pepper, and vinegar. Mix with crispy baguette pieces.

- Add in four bowls, top with parsley and tuna. Serve right away

Nutrition per serving: one cup: Calories 316|Saturated fat 1.5 g| Total carbohydrate 23 g| Sodium 171 mg | Total sugars 6 g| Total fat 10 g| Dietary fiber 6 g| Protein 19 g| Monounsaturated fat 5 g| Cholesterol 21 mg|

2. Shore Cream of Crab Soup

Preparation time: 10 minutes

Cook time: 25 minutes

Total time: 35 minutes

Serving: 4

Ingredients:

- 1 cup non-dairy creamer

- Unsalted butter: 1 tablespoon

- Old bay seasoning: 1/4 teaspoon

- 2 cups crab meat

- Chicken broth(low-sodium): 4 cups

- One medium onion

- Cornstarch: 2 tablespoons

- Black pepper: 1/8 teaspoon

- Dill weed: 1/8 teaspoon

Instructions:

- In a large pot, melt butter over medium flame.

- Add chopped onion to the pot. Cook until tender.

- Add crab meat—Cook for 2 to 3 minutes. Stir often.

- Add chicken broth, let it boil. Turn heat down to low.

- Mix starch and creamer in a bowl. Mix well.

- Add the mixture to the soup, increase the heat, stir until the soup thickens and gets to a boil.

- Add Old Bay, dill weed, pepper to soup.

Nutrition per serving: one cup: Calories 130 | Protein 12 g| carbohydrates 7 g| Fat 6 g| Cholesterol 53 mg| sodium 212 mg| Potassium 312 mg| Phosphorus 80 mg| Calcium 86 mg| Fiber 0.4 g

3. Pasta Salad with Mixed Vegetables

Preparation time: 10 minutes

Cook time: 30 minutes

Total time: 40 minutes

Serving: 8

Ingredients:

- Eight lettuce leaves, romaine
- One and a half cups of whole-wheat pasta, uncooked
- Olive oil: 1 tablespoon
- 1 clove of minced garlic
- 1 red, and one green bell pepper, cut into slices
- 2 onions, diced

- 3 and a half cups of tomato finely chopped, mash them a little

- Chicken broth, low-sodium: 1/4 cup

- 4 cups of mushrooms, sliced

- Oregano: half teaspoon

- Two zucchinis, shredded

- Basil: half teaspoon

Instructions:

- Cook pasta as per instructions, drain and add olive oil, mix well and set it aside.

- In a pan, add chicken broth, warm it through, add tomatoes, garlic and tomatoes.

- Cook for five minutes until transparent. Add the rest of the vegetables, until crispy tender for five more minutes. Add the oregano and basil.

- Add cooked vegetables to pasta, mix well.

- Keep in the refrigerator for one hour.

- Serve on top of lettuce leaves, and enjoy.

Nutrition per serving: two cups: Calories 251| Total carbohydrate 46 g| Sodium 60 mg| Dietary fiber 8 g| Total fat 3 g| Cholesterol Trace| Saturated fat 0.5 g| Protein 10 g| Total sugars 10 g| Monounsaturated fat 1.5 g|

4. Mango Tango Salad

Preparation time: 10 minutes

Cook time: 15 minutes

Total time: 30 minutes

Serving: 6

Ingredients:

- One Half of jalapeno pepper, chopped without seeds

- 3 large mangoes, cut into cubes

- Fresh cilantro leaves, chopped: 2 tablespoons

- Red onion, minced: 1 teaspoon

- Juice of one lime

Instructions:

- In a bowl, add all ingredients mix well.

- Let it rest for ten minutes.

- Toss again before serving.

Nutrition per serving: ½ cup: Calories 68| Sodium 10 mg| Total fat Trace| Cholesterol 0 mg| Protein 1 g |Total carbohydrate 16 g| Saturated fat Trace| Dietary fiber 2 g| Added sugars 0 g

5. Rotisserie Chicken Noodle Soup

Preparation time: 10 minutes

Cook time: 35 minutes

Total time: 45 minutes

Serving: 2-3

Ingredients:

- Carrots: 1 cup, sliced

- One cooked rotisserie chicken

- Half cup of onion, chopped

- Celery: 1 cup, sliced

- Chicken broth(low-sodium): 8 cups

- Fresh parsley: 3 tablespoons

- Wide noodles: 6 ounces, uncooked

Instructions:

- Take the bones out of the chicken and cut into one-inch pieces. Take four cups of chicken pieces.

- In a large pot, add chicken broth let it boil.

- Add noodles, chicken, and vegetables to the broth.

- Let it boil, and cook for 15 minutes. Make sure noodles are tender.

- Serve with chopped parsley on top.

Nutrition per serving: Calories 185| Protein 21 g| Carbohydrates 14 g| Fat 5 g| Cholesterol 63 mg| Sodium 361 mg| Potassium 294 mg| Phosphorus 161 mg | Calcium 22 mg| Fiber 1.4 g

6. Spring Vegetable Soup

Preparation time: 10 minutes

Cook time: 35 minutes

Total time: 45 minutes

Serving: 2-3

Ingredients:

- Vegetable broth(low-sodium): 4 cups
- Fresh green beans: 1 cup
- Half cup carrots
- Celery: 3/4 cup
- Garlic powder: 1 teaspoon
- Half cup onion
- Half cup mushrooms
- Olive oil: 2 tablespoons
- Dried oregano leaves: 1 teaspoon
- 1/4 teaspoon salt
- Half cup frozen corn

Instructions:

- Trim the green beans and chop into two-inch pieces
- Chop up the vegetables.
- In a pot, heat olive oil, sauté the onion and celery, till tender.

- Then add the remaining ingredients.

- Let it boil. Lower the heat, let it simmer.

- Cook for almost an hour.

Nutrition per serving: Calories 114| Protein 2 g| Carbohydrates 13 g| Fat 6 g| Cholesterol 0 mg| Sodium 262 mg| Potassium 365 mg| Phosphorus 108 mg| Calcium 48 mg| Fiber 3.4 g|

Chapter 8: Desserts Recipes

1. Fruit & Nut Bar

Preparation time: 10 minutes

Cook time: 30 minutes

Total time: 40 minutes

Serving: 24

Ingredients:

- Half cup of oats

- Flaxseed flour: 1/4 cup

- Cornstarch: 2 tablespoons

- Dried figs, chopped: 1/4 cup

- Half cup of quinoa flour

- Chopped almonds: 1/4 cup

- Dried apricots chopped: 1/4 cup

- 1/4 cup of honey

- Dried pineapple chopped: 1/4 cup

- Wheat germ: 1/4 cup

Instructions:

- Place parchment paper on a baking sheet. Add all ingredients, mix to combine. Make it

- into half-inch of thickness.

- Bake for 20 minutes, at 300 F.

- Cool it completely and slice into 24 pieces.

Nutrition per serving: Serving size: one bar: Calories 70| Total carbohydrate 11 g| Dietary fiber 2 g| Total fat 2 g| Sodium 4 mg| Cholesterol 0 mg| Protein 2 g| Added sugars 3 g| Monounsaturated fat 0.5 g| Total sugars 6 g| Saturated fat Trace|

2. Simple Brownies

Preparation time: 10 minutes

Cook time: 30 minutes

Total time: 40 minutes

Servings: 8

Ingredients:

- 6 ounces dark chocolate
- 4 eggs
- ½ cup hot water
- 1 teaspoon vanilla extract
- 2/3 cup coconut sugar
- 1 and ½ cups whole flour
- ½ cup walnuts chopped
- 1 teaspoon baking powder

Instructions:

- In a bowl, combine the chocolate and the hot water and whisk really well.
- Add vanilla extract and egg whites and whisk well again.
- In another bowl, combine the sugar with flour, baking powder and walnuts and stir.
- Combine the 2 mixtures, stir well, pour this into a cake pan greased with cooking spray, spread well, bake in the

oven for 30 minutes, cool down, slice and serve.

- Enjoy!

Nutrition per serving: Calories 144 | Total fat 4 g | Dietary fiber 4 g | Total carbohydrate 9 g | Protein 8 g

3. Baked Apples with Cherries & Almonds

Preparation time: 10 minutes

Cook time: 80 minutes

Total time: 90 minutes

Serving: 6

Ingredients:

- Chopped almonds: 3 tablespoons

- Wheat germ: 1 tablespoon

- 2 tablespoons of dark honey

- Dried cherries: 1/3 cup roughly chopped

- Ground cinnamon: half teaspoon

- Half cup of unsweetened apple juice

- Firmly packed: 1 tablespoon of brown sugar

- 1/8 teaspoon ground nutmeg

- 6 small-sized, golden apples

- 1/4 cup of water

- Canola oil: 2 teaspoons

Instructions:

- Let the oven preheat to 350 F.

- In a bowl, add almonds, brown sugar, cherries, nutmeg, cinnamon, and wheat germ. Mix well and set it aside.

- Peel or not peel the apples that are your preference.

- Make a cavity in the apple by removing the core.

- Add the cherry mixture to apples, placing firmly in the cavity.

- Place apples upright in a baking pan. Add water and apple juice to the pan.

- Pour oil and honey over apples. Cover with foil. Bake for 50-60 minutes until knife-tender.

- Serve warm or cold, drizzle apple juice on top, and serve.

Nutrition per serving: Serving size: 1 apple: Calories 200 | Total fat 4 g| Saturated fat 0 g| Total carbohydrate 39 g| Trans-fat 0 g| Added sugars 8 g| Monounsaturated fat 2 g| Cholesterol 0 mg| Dietary fiber 5 g| Total sugars 31 g| Protein 2 g| Sodium 7 mg|

4. Lemon Cheesecake

Preparation time: 10 minutes

Cook time: 60 minutes

Total time: 70 minutes

Serving: 8

Ingredients:

- 1 packet of unflavored gelatin
- 2 tablespoons of fresh lemon juice
- Half cup of skim milk, heated enough to almost boiling
- Coldwater: 2 tablespoons
- 1 teaspoon of vanilla extract
- 2 large egg whites

- Cottage cheese, low-fat: 2 cups
- Grated Lemon zest
- 1/4 cup of honey or sugar

Instructions:

- In a food blender, add lemon juice, water, and gelatin. Pulse on low for one or 2 minutes, until gelatin softens.

- Add warmed milk to dissolve gelatin. Add honey, egg whites, cheese, and vanilla to the blender. Pulse on high until smooth.

- Take a round pie plate of 9 inches. Pour the mixture into it. Chill in the fridge for 2-3 hours.

- Serve with lemon zest on top, and enjoy.

Nutrition per serving: Serving size: 1/8 of a cake: Calories 80| Total carbohydrate 9 g| Sodium 252 mg| Added sugars 9 g | Saturated fat Trace| Dietary fiber Trace| Cholesterol 3 mg| Protein 9 g| Monounsaturated fat Trace| Trans-fat 0 g| Total fat 1 g|

5. Cinnamon Apples

Preparation time: 10 minutes

Cook time: 20 minutes

Total time: 30 minutes

Servings: 4

Ingredients:

- 4 big apples

- 4 tablespoons raisins

- 1 tablespoon cinnamon powder

Instructions:

- Stuff the apples with the raisins, sprinkle the cinnamon, arrange them in a baking dish, introduce in the oven at 375 degrees F, bake for 20 minutes and serve cold.

- Enjoy!

Nutrition per serving: Calories 200 g | Total fat 3 g | Dietary fiber 4 | Total carbohydrate 8 g | Protein 5 g

6. Fruit Cake

Preparation time: 10 minutes

Cook time: 45 minutes

Total time: 55 minutes

Serving: 12

Ingredients:

- Apple juice, unsweetened: half cup

- Unsweetened applesauce: half cup

- Crushed pineapple: half cup of packed in juice, drained

- Zest and juice of 1 lemon

- Assorted dried fruit: 2 cups such as chopped dates, cherries, and currants

- Real vanilla extract: 2 tablespoons

- Juice and zest of 1 medium-sized orange

- 1/4 cup of honey

- Half cup of rolled oats

- Low sodium baking soda: half teaspoon

- Flaxseed flour: 1/4 cup

- Baking powder: half teaspoon

- Whole-wheat: 1 cup pastry flour

- Half cup of chopped walnuts

- 1 whole egg

Instructions:

- In a mixing bowl, add applesauce, juices, dried fruit, fruit zests, vanilla, and pineapple. Mix well and let it rest for 15-20 minutes.

- Take a 9x4" baking pan, place parchment paper on the bottom.

- In a bowl, add flours, honey, baking soda, oats, and baking powder. Mix well. Add fruits. Add wet ingredients to dry ingredients. Mix to combine.

- Add walnuts and eggs, and stir well.

- Pour mixture into the prepared loaf pan, and bake for one hour at 325 F, or if the toothpick is inserted, it should come out clean.

- Let the cake cool for half an hour before taking it out from the pan.

- Slice and serve.

Nutrition per serving: Serving size: one slice, one loaf cut into 12 pieces: Calories 229| Total carbohydrate 41 g| Sodium 117 mg| Total fat 5 g| Dietary fiber 5 g| Cholesterol 15 mg| Protein 5 g| Added sugars 5 g| Monounsaturated fat 1 g| Total sugars 25 g

Chapter 9: DASH Diet Bonus

1. Baby Spinach Snack

Preparation time: 10 minutes

Cooking time: 10 minutes

Total time: 20 minutes

Servings: 3

Ingredients:
- 2 cups baby spinach
- A pinch of black pepper
- ½ tablespoon olive oil
- ½ teaspoon garlic powder

Instructions:
- Spread the baby spinach on a lined baking sheet, add oil, black pepper and garlic powder, toss a bit, introduce in the oven, bake at 350 degrees F for 10 minutes, divide into bowls and serve as a snack.
- Enjoy!

Nutrition per serving: Calories 125 g | Total fat 4 g | Total fiber 1 g | Total carbohydrate 4 | Protein 2 g

2. Red Bean Soup

Preparation time: 10 minutes

Cooking time: 1 hour and 45 minutes

Total time: 1 hour and 55 minutes

Servings: 4

Ingredients:

- 1-pound red kidney beans, soaked overnight and drained
- 8 cups water
- ¾ cup low-sodium beef stock
- 1 green bell pepper, chopped

- 1 tomato, chopped
- 1 yellow onion, chopped
- 3 garlic cloves, minced
- 1 chili pepper, chopped
- 1-pound beef brisket, cubed
- 1 potato, cubed
- A pinch of black pepper

Instructions:

- Put the water and the stock in a pot and heat up over medium heat.
- Add beans, bell pepper, tomato, onion, garlic, chili pepper and beef, stir and simmer for 1 hour and 30 minutes.
- Add potato and a pinch of black pepper, stir, cook for 15 minutes more, divide into bowls and serve for lunch.
- Enjoy!

Nutrition per serving: Calories 221 g |Total fat 7 g |Total fiber 8 g |Total carbohydrate 18 g | Protein 8 g

3. Sautéed Fresh Corn

Preparation time: 10 minutes

Cook time: 20 Minutes

Total time: 30 minutes

Serving: 6

Ingredients:

- Corn kernels, fresh: 2 cups

- Olive oil: 1 teaspoon

- Minced garlic: 1 teaspoon

- 4 tbsp. Of ham, sliced into thin strips

- One green bell pepper, chopped, without seeds

Instructions:

- In a pan, sauté the ham in olive oil on medium flame, for five minutes, or until crispy.

- Add in garlic and bell pepper, cook for 5-7 minutes, until the kernel is tender.

- Serve hot and enjoy.

Nutrition per serving: 3/4 cup: Calories 78|| Total sugars 4 g| Total carbohydrate 11 g| Sodium 216 mg| Dietary fiber 1 g| Saturated fat 0.5 g| Cholesterol 8 mg| Total fat 2 g | Protein 4 g

4. Easy Vegetable Stock

Preparation time: 10 minutes

Cook time: 35 Minutes

Total time: 45 minutes

Serving: 6

Ingredients:

- Water: 8 cups
- Olive oil: 3 teaspoons
- One yellow onion, sliced into one-inch pieces
- Six cloves of garlic, cut in half
- Three large carrots, cut into one-inch pieces
- 4 thyme sprigs, 1/8 teaspoon
- Two stalks of celery with leaves, sliced into one-inch pieces

- White mushrooms: 12 to 14 fresh cleaned and roughly chopped
- 6 sprigs of flat-leaf fresh parsley
- One bay leaf
- Salt: 1/8 teaspoon

Instructions:

- In a pot, sauté mushroom in two tbsp. of olive oil, until browned, for 4 to 5 minutes. Take mushrooms out, add garlic, carrots, celery, and onions, sauté for six minutes, add mushrooms and cook for 1 to 2 minutes. Brown the vegetables.
- Add salt, parsley, bay leaf, water, and thyme. Let it boil, turn the heat low, and let it simmer for half an hour, uncovered.
- Turn off the heat and slightly cool the broth.
- Strain the stock, use right away, and keep in the fridge for three days.

Nutrition per serving: one cup: Calories 22|Total fat 2.3 g| Cholesterol 0 g| Sodium 93.2 mg| Total carbohydrate 1.2 g| Dietary fiber 0 g| sugars 0 g| Protein 0 g

5. Yellow Lentils with Spinach & Ginger

Preparation time: 10 minutes

Cook time: 30 Minutes

Total time: 40 minutes

Serving: 4

Ingredients:

- Chopped, stemmed, baby spinach leaves: 2 cups
- Olive oil: 1 tablespoon
- Ground ginger: 1 teaspoon
- Curry powder: half teaspoon
- Vegetable stock: 1 and a half cups, no-salt-added
- Ground turmeric: half teaspoon
- 2 tablespoons minced onion
- Yellow lentils: 1 cup cleaned, rinsed, drained
- Light coconut milk: half cup
- 1/4 teaspoon salt

For Serving:

- Fresh cilantro: 1 tablespoon
- Sesame seeds, white or black: 1 teaspoon

Instructions:

- In a large pan, sauté onion, curry powder, ginger, and turmeric in olive oil, cook for one minute or two.

- Add coconut milk and lentils on a medium-high flame, let it boil, turn the heat down, and let it simmer for 12 minutes. If it's too thick, add some water.

- Toast the sesame seeds on medium flame, stirring constantly.

- Add spinach to the lentils, cover it and let it simmer for three minutes.

- Add in the salt if you like. Top with sesame seeds and fresh cilantro, serve right away.

Nutrition per serving: 3/4 cup: Calories 263| Sodium 348 mg |Total carbohydrate 36 g| Saturated fat 2 g| Total sugars 4 g | Total fat 7 g| Dietary fiber 16 g | Cholesterol 0 mg| Protein 14 g

Chapter 10: Sauces & Dressings

1. Grilled Mango Chutney

Preparation time: 10 minutes

Cook time: 10 minutes

Total time: 20 minutes

Serving: 6

Ingredients:

- One mango
- Fresh rosemary chopped: 1/4 teaspoon
- Honey: 1/4 cup
- Cider vinegar: 2 tablespoons
- Finely chopped green bell pepper: 2 tablespoons
- Chopped red onion: 1/4 cup
- Grated fresh ginger: 1 tablespoon
- Half teaspoon of ground ginger
- Ground cloves: 1/8 teaspoon

Instructions:

- Preheat the charcoal grill, place the greased rack 4-6 inches away from the heat source.
- Grill the mango on medium heat for three minutes on every side. Or broil if you do not have a grill.

- Let the mango cool, cut into bite-size pieces.

- Add the rest of the ingredients and mix.

- Chill for one hour and serve.

Nutrition per serving: Serving size: 2 half tablespoons: Calories 58|Cholesterol 0 mg| Sodium 1 mg| Total fat Trace| Total carbohydrate 15 g| Saturated fat Trace| Dietary fiber 1 g| Trans-fat 0 g| Added sugars 8 g

2. Squash Salsa

Preparation time: 10 minutes

Cook time: 13 minutes

Total time: 23 minutes

Servings: 6

Ingredients:

- 3 tablespoons olive oil
- 5 medium squash, peeled and sliced
- 1 cup pepitas
- Toasted 7 tomatillos
- A pinch of black pepper

- 1 small onion
- Chopped 2 tablespoons fresh lime juice
- 2 tablespoons cilantro chopped

Instructions:

- Heat up a pan over medium heat, add tomatillos, onion and black pepper, stir, cook for 3 minutes
- transfer to your food processor and pulse
- Add lime juice and cilantro, pulse again and transfer to a bowl
- 3. Heat up your kitchen grill over high heat, drizzle the oil over squash slices, grill them for 10 minutes
- divide them between plates, add pepitas and tomatillos mix on top and serve as a side dish
- Enjoy!

Nutrition per serving: Calories 263| Sodium 348 mg |Total carbohydrate 36 g| Saturated fat 2 g| Total sugars 4 g | Total fat 7 g| Dietary fiber 16 g | Cholesterol 0 mg| Protein 14 g

Conclusion

I want to personally thank you for getting my book, and I would be very grateful if you could leave your honest review about this book. I certainly want to thank you in advance for doing this.
Eating good and healthy food is not only possible, it is also simple, you just need to know the food.

This amazing lifestyle will change your life forever and it will transform you into a happier and healthier person in no time!

Eating is essential and science helps us to choose what to eat in order to keep healthy, but we must not forget that a healthy diet is also varied and appetizing. It can be the occasion for something good for oneself, and also to experience new flavors and to share with someone the pleasure of preparing and eating a tasty dish.

Enjoy your meal, but even before that, enjoy smart shopping and have fun in the kitchen!

CPSIA information can be obtained
at www.ICGtesting.com
Printed in the USA
BVHW092053080621
609008BV00003B/537